S0-DYE-195

Bridget,

To my Birthday

Buckley! I love you, kid.

I'm so proud to have

you as my niece! Thanks

for being part of my life day!

Suzie

Bridget

A Gift To

Suzie

From

Aug. 26, 2006

On This Date

HAPPY Birthday!

a celebration of you

A DAYMAKER GREETING BOOK

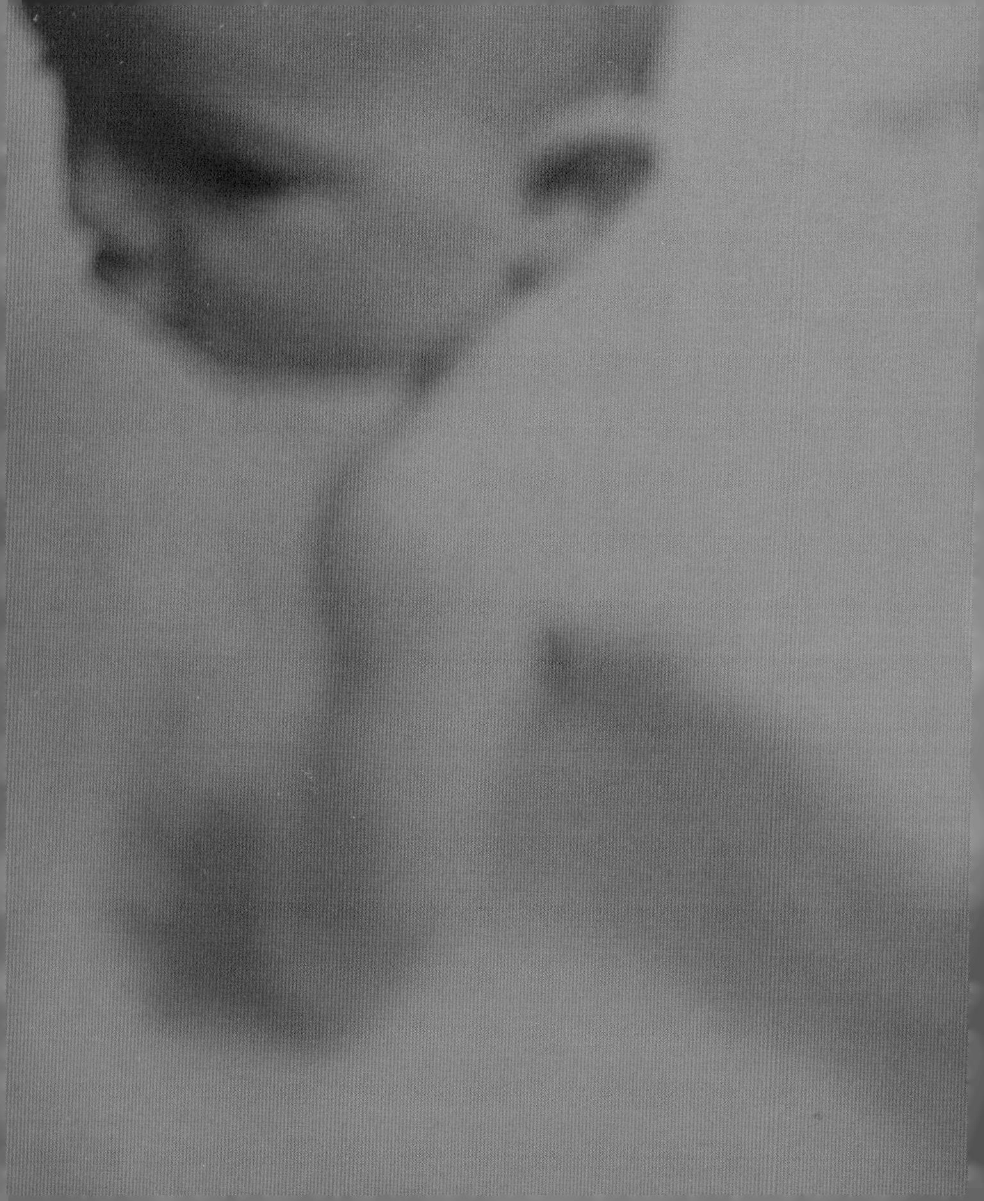

THIS IS YOUR DAY.

THE SPECIAL DAY OF YOUR ARRIVAL

INTO THE WORLD.

(YOU CAME SPECIAL DELIVERY)

A GIFT FROM ABOVE.

RECEIVED BY ALL WHO KNOW YOU.

TODAY AND ALWAYS,

BLESSINGS AND PRAYERS

FOR THE CHAPTERS

OF YOUR LIFE WHICH HAVE

YET TO BE WRITTEN.

Happy Bir

happy birthday to you!

hday to You!

(HAPPY BIRTHDAY, OH DEAR ONE)

HAPPY BIRTHDAY

TO YOU!

I'm so glad God made you.

God is still creating the world, you know, adding details, perfecting, creating entire new things that no one has ever seen before. And we are each part of His creation. Nor are our births the end of the story—look into your own heart and you will see all the amazing things He is creating, if you will only let Him.

And I, for one, am glad, glad, glad—not only that God made you, but that He continues to make you, year after year.

LUCIE CHRISTOPHER

You Are

Special!

Why is it that children celebrate each birthday milestone with joy and triumph—but some adults go into mourning (mock or real) as each milestone arrives? The reason has to do, I think, with our culture's attitude about growing older. Up to about age twenty-five, the added years are welcomed—but for the remaining fifty or sixty years of our lives, we act as though the passage of time were a sad secret, a source of shame and regret.

How silly! Celebrate your years. Be grateful for all the gifts time has given you. God has meaning and purpose for each season of your life—and with each birthday milestone, you can celebrate all He's taught you. After all, in Christ, little by little, year by year, God transforms you into His image.

THERE IS NO ONE ELSE LIKE YOU

God's creation is lavish—such detailed beauty, so many creatures, such lovely abundance. His delight in His creation never tires, as moment by moment He continues to design snowflakes and DNA cells, supernovas and galaxies, no two alike, each one unique and special.

You, too, are a part of God's creation, a special and essential part of His plan for our world. No one else can take your place. No one else can be you.

I'm so glad God created you!

Our birth is but a sleep and a forgetting:
The soul that rises with us, our life's star,
Hath had elsewhere its setting,
And cometh from afar:
Not in entire forgetfulness,
And not in utter nakedness,
But trailing clouds of glory do we come
From God, who is our home.

WILLIAM WORDSWORTH

Many, O LORD my God, are the wonders you have done. The things you planned for us no one can recount to you; were I to speak and tell of them, they would be too many to declare.

PSALM 40:5 NIV

Birthday Milestones

There is something satisfying, rejuvenating, comforting about the seasons. They remind me that I play one small part in a much bigger picture—that there is a pulse, a sequence, a journey set into motion by the very hand of God Himself.

KAREN SCALF LINAMEN

Thine hands
have made me
and fashioned
me together
round about.
JOB 10:8 KJV

You Are

Unique!

You are a part

of the great plan,

an indispensable part.

You are needed;

you have your own

unique share in the

freedom of Creation.

MADELEINE L'ENGLE

The way you are put together is unique—different from any other. Even identical twins can be distinguished by voice or mannerisms. God has designed you wonderfully well. He thinks about you every minute of every day. He has a special purpose just for you, a niche that only you can fill. Remember, on this special day, you are loved!

LORI SHANKLE

I praise you because I am fearfully and wonderfully made;
your works are wonderful, I know that full well.
My frame was not hidden from you when I was made
in the secret place. When I was woven together
in the depths of the earth, your eyes saw my unformed
body. All the days ordained for me were written
in your book before one of them came to be.

Psalm 139:14-18 NIV

God Made Today Just for You

My heart is full
of gratitude,
today and always,
for all that
you mean to me!

BLOOM AND BE FRUITFUL

Our culture's obsession with youth is skewed. Why did we ever get the idea that our worth diminishes with the passing years? After all, look at the natural world. The mature plants, not the immature, are the ones that flower and yield fruit.

With each passing year, may you see your life bursting into fresh bloom, yielding a richer and richer harvest of the Spirit's fruit.

The fruit of the Spirit
is love, joy, peace,
longsuffering, gentleness,
goodness, faith,
meekness, temperance.

GALATIANS 5:22-23

Flowers preach to us
if we will hear.

CHRISTINA ROSSETTI

You Ar

Loved!

What would I have done
if God hadn't made you?
The world wouldn't
have been the same.
All the talks that we've had,
all the laughter we've shared,
could not be replaced,
by fortune nor fancy nor fame.

ALEXANDRA ELIZONDO

Birthday months marked by special gems and flowers:

- *January: garnet and carnation*
- *February: amethyst and violet*
- *March: aquamarine and jonquil*
- *April: diamond and sweet pea*
- *May: emerald and lily of the valley*
- *June: pearl and rose*
- *July: ruby and larkspur*
- *August: peridot and gladiolus*
- *September: sapphire and aster*
- *October: opal and calendula*
- *November: topaz and chrysanthemum*
- *December: turquoise and narcissus*

A Party in Heaven

There's a birthday song for children that goes something like this: "On the day you were born, an angel shouted and blew on his horn." I can just imagine the scene in heaven, everyone shouting and clapping, a riot of music filling the heavenly vault, smiles on each celestial face—all because you were born!

The angels still celebrate your birth. So do I—and so does God.

I thank my God upon every remembrance of you.

PHILIPPIANS 1:3

Celeb

ate!

The Gift That Flies

Dost thou love life?

Then do not

squander time,

for that's the stuff

life is made of.

BENJAMIN FRANKLIN

Let time flow by,
with which we flow on
to be transformed
into the glory of
the children of God.

FRANCIS DE SALES

You are never too old
to set another goal
or to dream a new dream.

LES BROWN

✶

Time is the herald of Truth.

ELIZABETH GRYMESTON

✶

As if you could kill time
without injuring eternity.

HENRY DAVID THOREAU

Birth may
be a matter
of a moment,
but it is a
unique one.
FREDERICK
LEBOYER

MY WISH FOR YOU

On your birthday, as you look at your life, may you rejoice in all the years have brought you—and may you recognize the fruit of the Spirit ripening year by year. I especially wish you the bright, sweet fruits of joy and peace and love.

One thing I'd give my friend,
If I could give you one thing,
I would wish for you the ability
To see yourself as others see you.
Then you would realize what
a truly special person you are.

B. A. BILLINGSLY

The here-and-now is no mere filling of time,
but a filling of time with God.
JOHN FOSTER

I am the vine, ye are the branches:
He that abideth in me, and I in him,
the same bringeth forth much fruit.
JOHN 15:5

I have chosen you, and ordained
you, that ye should go and
bring forth fruit, and that
your fruit should remain.
JOHN 15:16

Make use of time,
let not advantage slip;
Beauty within itself
should not be wasted.
WILLIAM
SHAKESPEARE

Divin

e Gifts

Simple Joys

With time, we often lose a child's knack for simply being happy. And with so many responsibilities we almost feel guilty if we feel joyful, as though we don't deserve to be so happy.

But joy is one of God's gifts, the fruit of the Spirit at work in your life. So on this special day and all year long—rejoice! Be glad! Celebrate!

Things Precious

Time is wonderful gift given to us by God—so don't fear the passing years. Celebrate them! The best things in life, the truly precious things, get better with time; each year only increases their value.

Your life is like that, too. For each year that I know you, I appreciate you more and more. I'm so thankful for your life.

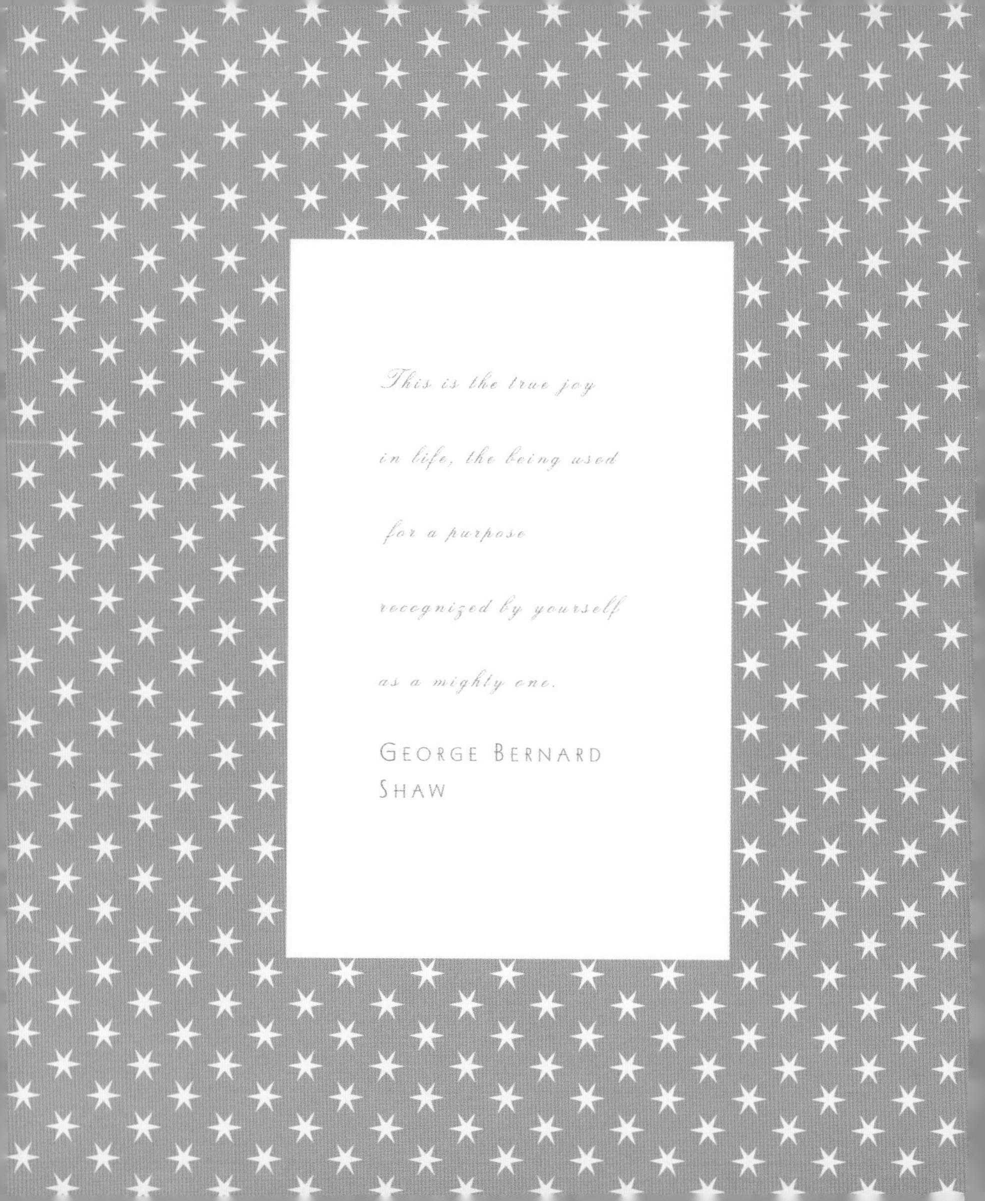
This is the true joy
in life, the being used
for a purpose
recognized by yourself
as a mighty one.
GEORGE BERNARD
SHAW

I desire fruit that may
abound to your account.
PHILIPPIANS 4:17 KJV

*

Be patient therefore. . . .
Behold, the husbandman
waiteth for the precious
fruit of the earth, and hath
long patience for it,
until he receive the early
and latter rain.
Be ye also patient. . . .
JAMES 5:7-8

Joy is not in things, it is in us.
RICHARD WAGNER

Often we see life as a series of mundane things—chores that must be accomplished, errands that must be run—and we forget that each moment that passes is a gift given to us by God. When you look back on the years God has ordained for you, what will you see? I pray that you will be able to find joy and beauty in the most trivial of things, because you have spent those precious minutes with God.

LORI SHANKLE

How fit to employ
All the heart and the soul
and the senses forever in joy!

ROBERT BROWNING

With. . .the deep power of joy,

we see into the life of things.

WILLIAM WORDSWORTH

*

Ask, and ye shall receive,

that your joy may be full.

JOHN 16:24

*

Happiness is not a possession to be prized,

it is a quality of thought,

a state of mind.

DAPHNE DU MAURIER

*

The art of being happy lies in the power

of extracting happiness from common things.

HENRY WARD BEECHER

Happiness is as a butterfly, which,
when pursued, is always beyond our grasp,
but which, if you will sit down quietly,
may alight upon you.

NATHANIEL HAWTHORNE

Let all thy joys be as the month of May,
And all thy days be as a marriage day:
Let sorrow, sickness, and a troubled mind
Be stranger to thee.

FRANCIS QUARLES

Make use of time, let not advantage slip;
Beauty within itself should not be wasted.

WILLIAM SHAKESPEARE

The best and most
beautiful things
in the world cannot
be seen or even touched.
They must be felt
with the heart.
HELEN KELLER

A Birthday Blessing

MAY THE GOD

OF HOPE, FILL YOU

WITH ALL JOY AND PEACE

AS YOU TRUST IN HIM

SO THAT YOU MAY

OVERFLOW WITH HOPE

BY THE POWER OF

THE HOLY SPIRIT.

ROMANS 15:12-14

Happy Birthday (DayMaker gift book)
by Ellyn Sanna

ISBN 1-58660-709-X

Cover photo ©Megumi Ono/Photonica

Previously released as *Happy Birthday: A Celebration of You!*

All Scripture quotations, unless otherwise noted, are taken from the King James Version of the Bible.

Published by Barbour Books, an imprint of Barbour Publishing, Inc., P. O. Box 719, Uhrichsville, Ohio 44683, www.barbourbooks.com

Printed in China.